> The "elderly"
> seem so much younger
> than they used to be!

*Age doesn't matter
unless you're a cheese.*
　　　　　— *Billie Burke*

*Age is like underwear —
it creeps up on you.*

*The reason most women don't tell their age
is because most men don't act theirs!*

"Older" is when you feel your oats less,
and your corns more.

It's a good day when I wake up ~ and nothing new hurts.

The best way to tell a woman's age is when she's not around.

A woman's age is her own business; and most women certainly know how to mind their own business.

Getting older is when we would rather not have a good time than have to get over it.

— *Oscar Wilde*

Wife of recent retiree:
   *"I know we married for better or worse —
   but not for lunch!"*

*He had known her for many years;
in fact,
ever since they were the same age.*

Women age quicker than men, but less often.

The "elderly" are always those 15 years older than I am.

— Bernard Baruch

*The older the violin
the sweeter the tune.*

No wise man ever wished to be younger.

— *Jonathan Swift*

*Age and understanding
will overcome youth and skill.*

*Age readily undertakes tasks that youth shirks,
because they would take too long.*

— Somerset Maugham

At 78 Grandma Moses began to paint.

At 81 Benjamin Franklin was the mediator responsible for the Constitution of the United States becoming a reality.

At 59 Michelangelo painted the Last Judgment on the altar wall of the Sistine Chapel.

At 65 Winston Churchill took on the largest job of the first half of this century — the defeat of Nazism.

*As soon as you feel too old to do a thing,
do it.*

— *Margaret Deland*

There is nothing more remarkable in the life of Socrates than that he found time in his old age to learn to dance and play on instruments, and thought it time well spent.
— Montaigne

*It's not how old we are,
but how we are old.*

We are always the same age inside.
— Gertrude Stein

It is always in season for men to learn.

—*Aeschyhus*

As a man advances (matures) he gets something better than admiration — judgment to estimate things at their own value.

— Samuel Johnson

*As the old rooster crows
the young rooster learns.*

There are no young sages.

The older we get the more we balance passion with compassion.

*The more senior
   the more seasoned.*

— *van R*

(Seasoned: made fit by experience.)

...take all the experience and judgment of men over fifty out of the world and there won't be enough left to run it.

— Henry Ford

Fire is seen in the eyes of the young,
but it is light that we see
in the eyes of the seasoned.

— Victor Hugo

To be seventy years young is often
far more cheerful
than to be forty years old.
— Oliver Wendell Holmes

No Spring, nor Summer beauty
hath such grace
as I have seen in one Autumnal face.
— John Donne

*Come, grow old along with me —
the best is yet to be.*

— *Browning*